AMBER ROYER

The Thoughtful Travel Journal

GOLDEN TIP PRESS

GOLDEN TIP PRESS

A Golden Tip Press paperback original 2024

Copyright © Amber Royer 2024

Distributed in the United States by Ingram, Tennessee

All rights reserved. Amber Royer asserts the moral right to be identified as the author of this work.

Sale of this book without a front cover may be unauthorized. If this book is coverless, it may have been reported as "unsold and destroyed" and neither the author nor the publisher may have received payment for it.

ISBN 978-1-952854-22-4

Printed in the United States of America

Also by Amber Royer:

Grand Openings Can Be Murder

70% Dark Intentions

Out of Temper

A Shot in the 80 Percent Dark

A Study in Chocolate

Something Borrowed, Something 90% Dark

A Chocolate is Announced

Free Chocolate

Pure Chocolate

Fake Chocolate

Story Like a Journalist

There Are Herbs in My Chocolate

Travel Journaling

"I never travel without my diary. One should always have something sensational to read on the train." – Oscar Wilde

Journaling is the most basic free-form version of writing about yourself. You can use whatever format you choose and you don't have to worry about structure. Just let the ideas flow. No one has to see inside your journal unless you let them. You can be your most honest, authentic self. You can also see how that authentic self has changed and grown over time by keeping a record. Journaling provides a number of psychological benefits, some of which come from the act of organizing your thoughts and finding a routine – but others which come from embracing writing as an act of catharsis.

Travel journaling is a more specific form of journaling, which involves recording thoughts and impressions about a specific time and place, while you are in the moment. It provides a record to look back on, when the sharp edges of the experience have started to fade, and helps provide meaning to the travel experience.

This journal is meant to help you organize those thoughts and create a very personal keepsake. It is also beneficial for someone who wants to plan a travel blog, or to turn the experience into a memoir, or fiction set in the places you have traveled. I encourage you to read through the instructional text, and decide how you want to approach journaling, before your next trip. Of course, if you have a vision for your journal, and all you need is the space for writing, go for it! After all, a journal can be whatever helps you.

Traveling with Purpose

We often travel for pleasure or business, but sometimes there is a purpose to the journey itself. Finding a purpose for your journey can connect you to the world – and to travel journal writers who have gone before.

There's a long history of using travel journals to document scientific discovery and exploration. Lewis and Clarke, Captain Cook and Charles Darwin kept detailed records of their voyages – and, despite their complicated personal legacies, their observations went on to become the foundational text for study by individuals in a number of fields. More recently, Jacques Cousteau thoroughly documented his exploration of the world's marine environments. Along the way, he invented SCUBA equipment and set up a non-profit society to bring awareness to the plight of the world's oceans. All because he went into the water one day wearing goggles and saw the wonderous world beneath. His guiding philosophy can be summed up in the quote, "We must go and see for ourselves." In other words: you can't love the ocean if you know nothing about it.

Even Gordon Ramsey, with his Uncharted series, has created basically a visual travel journal as he journeys around the world, learning how people grow, catch, and cook food in different areas. He's risked his life collecting goose barnacles from the rocky coastline in Portugal, and learned new skills pulling up lobster pots in Maine – and he's sharing the recipes to prove it. Even some of his early shows emphasized his goal of teaching average folks where their food comes from, so his take in Uncharted makes perfect sense and gives him the reason to ask questions, interact with experts and eat good food.

You don't have to set out with anything so grand in mind to travel with purpose. Maybe you want to expand your horizons and learn about life in a different part of the world. Or maybe you're on a personal journey of healing and self-discovery, traveling to push yourself out of your comfort zone.

Personal journeys likewise have a long history. In the 17th and 18th centuries, Europeans who had the means to travel sometimes engaged in "The Grand Tour." The purpose was education and self-improvement, and was in some ways connected to coming of age. Participants traveled across Europe – and sometimes beyond – investigating art, architecture and antiquities. They were usually accompanied by a tutor, and it was expected that the journey would inspire some type of writing or art – be it song, poetry or painting. (They also brought home mementos, creating perhaps the world's first significant market for non-religious travel souvenirs. Other souvenir traditions had grown out of pilgrimages and similar journeys. For example, the Japanese tradition of Omiyage – bringing small gifts to friends and co-workers from the places you have traveled – are thought to originate from pilgrims visiting shrines and bringing home proof that they had made it to the location. Over time, this broadened to include secular travel, and Japanese people started bringing back delicacies that represented the region they had visited.) While a Grand Tour often lasted a year or more, you can build a travel journal a bit at a time, with shorter trips, chronicling how you have changed and grown from your travel experiences at each destination you have visited, throughout the period of your life covered by the journal.

You can also have more than one purpose for a trip. Personally, I Instagram and Youtube about my travels, so I always make sure to include visual components, photographing things that may or may not be immediately useful. But I also write fiction, and even if my travel isn't directly related to a book I'm working on, I find that tidbits of people and places, along with random facts I wouldn't otherwise have thought to find out, wind up in my work – even years later. My own travel journaling often takes the form of random notes on things I didn't know about an area, or details on various processes (often related to food and beverages, or sometimes technology.) I know how something works, or what it really looks like, because I took a tour, visited a museum, or asked a question. Simply being a writer gives my travel multiple purposes. The simple fact of keeping a journal may help do the same for you.

Looking at the journalistic 5Ws and H – who, what, when, where, how and why – the last one – WHY – is perhaps the most important. A journalistic article can have interesting quotes and salacious details, but without a purpose, a WHY that gives it context, it all falls flat. WHY as a reader, should I care? WHY should I take action? WHY should I change the way I feel about something?

The WHY can be less straightforward in travel journaling, but in order to create something meaningful, even if you don't plan to share the journal with anyone but yourself, the WHY has to be there.

Travelogues and Fiction – Twain vs. Michener

A travel journal can be used as notes for creating a full-fledged travelogue. Travelogues are usually written in first person and recounted in the past tense. Because you have in effect become the main character of your travelogue, you lend your voice to it, and it is filtered through your narrative point of view. This makes the resulting work more personal than anything achieved in a guidebook or non-fiction work on a particular destination. Travelogues allow for the inclusion of specific non-repeatable experiences, alongside instruction about culture and history. You might share your reasons for traveling to the place (which may or may not feel universal to your readers) and encourage others to visit for reasons of their own. It all needs to come together into a seamless narrative with beginning and end points of setting off on your adventure, bookended with your return.

One of the most famous travelogues is Mark Twain's *Innocents Abroad*, which mixes humor with more serious content involving history and culture as Twain traveled across Europe, even poking fun at tourists who merely follow guidebooks. Reading it, you can clearly see a specific perspective, capturing a personal take on a specific trip the author took in 1867. Yet, it was written with a universal enough appeal that it is still in print.

If you want to create your own travelogue, structure your story either thematically or chronologically. Imagine yourself as the protagonist of a story, and give your journey through the place you visited a beginning, middle and end. Think about details that will help set your story in a specific time and place, so that if someone were to pick up the manuscript a hundred years from now, it would have a universal appeal, but contain enough specific facts and impressions to transport the reader back in time.

-Start in a place that sets the mood for your travelogue, whether it be humorous or philosophical. When you remember the place you've traveled to, what's the first concrete image that comes into your head? Can that object encapsulate the mood of the place? Try to describe it in a way where we pick up on the mood without you having to overtly state it.

-Or start with a conflict or problem that introduces tension.

-Use your journal to pick out details to include in the piece. It can be helpful for remembering the names of people and locations, in case you need to reach out for permissions, or to ask for additional information. A travelogue may focus on impressions, but it should still be factually accurate.

-End with a lesson, a discovery or a personal transformation.

In some cases, you may wish to transmute your experiences into fiction. Travel stories can be simi-autobiographical and based on your travel journal. By making the work fiction, it becomes much easier to line up events so that there is a story with a beginning, middle and ending. You can change the facts to fit with your story's theme, or re-order events so that they make more sense for your protagonist's character arc. You can turn a chance meeting into a lifelong friendship, or change a decision you made to explore the "if only" you had taken another path.

Or, you may simply be inspired by the place you have visited, or by someone you met, to write a fictional story set in that place or around that character. The biggest consideration here is showing respect for the place you've visited and the people you've met.

Mark Twain also wrote a series of letters as a young reporter assigned to cover Hawaii, that were later collected into a book. They're raucous and funny, and say as much about a young reporter having too much fun in Maui to meet deadline as they do about the times and now-history he was covering. James Michener, on the other hand, moved to Waikiki in 1958 and partnered with local scholar Clarice Taylor, to research his book Hawaii. Though there is much folklore woven into the book, the historic parts are accurate. Michener paints a complicated picture of Hawaii that rings authentic due to the tremendous amount of work he put into showing multiple viewpoints with characters from different cultures. The book is a multi-generational epic. It would have been impossible to insert himself as narrator, and limit the research to just one trip – as did Twain, in his book of letters. But Michener was clearly inspired by what he saw and the people he interacted with.

If you want create your own work of fiction from your travel journal:

-Start with a hook, a little bit of conflict that asks a WHY question that we need answered. In a novel-length work, this leads to a plot question that forms the core of the book's plot. Can Mari find love on her summer vacation? Will the spies make it off the island before the volcano erupts? Will Gregor uncover the secret hidden at the Louvre? In a short story, this is all simplified, but there should still be an uncertainty we as readers want to see resolved. That's what keeps us turning pages.

-Introduce complications that make it seem impossible that the plot question will be resolved. Test your characters' flaws and put obstacles in their way that make them fight to resolve the question.

-Be sure to include a moment where it looks like your characters have failed. This allows your protagonist to arc, becoming a

better (or occasionally worse) version of herself, with the clarity to find the solution to the plot question.

-Include an overarching theme. If you want your story to be memorable, it has to mean something, and theme is how you communicate that to a reader. Keep it subtle, but recognizable throughout.

-Come back at the end to an image or theme from the beginning. Give us a clear answer to the plot question (Yes, Mari found love and is now moving to Italy) and a brief thought about how the experience has dealt with her personal flaws and helped her grow as a person (she has stopped being obsessed with schedules and perfectionism, and is now embracing a seasonal pace for life as she opens a winery).

The Pillow Book: Journals as literature

Even in their original form, journals have at times become literature. One moving journal that many of us have read is The Diary of Anne Frank (*The Diary of a Young Girl*). Anne was an ordinary girl dealing with horrifically impossible circumstances. Her diary wasn't meant to be literature, and she would surely have been astounded to learn of the influence her journaling has had on the world. The book is included in several lists of the most important books of the 20th Century. Truly, journals can serve as examples (or warning examples) to others, on how to deal with social pressures, grasp opportunities – or deal with difficult times.

In 10th century Japan, an even older journal actually shaped the course of that country's literature. Sei Shonagon, a lady in waiting to Empress Sadako decided to keep a "pillow book." (Shonagnon is a title, Sei is likely a family name.) Pillow books were journals that court ladies kept hidden inside stone or wooden pillows (more of a structured neck support than the soft pillows we think of today). According to many resources, It was meant to be private writing, but one day she accidentally left the book out on a cushion, and a visiting guest carried it away. It was handed around at court, then copied as handwritten manuscripts, then eventually published as a book in the 17th century. (It has been edited in several different ways, with some of the entries in different order.)

This was the start of zuihitsu literature, which consists of loosely connected personal essays and fragmented ideas. It took off in the Japanese court, and gained mainstream popularity by the Edo era. It was still relevant enough at that time that a parody, *The Dog Pillow*, was published. Even Japanese scholars began writing in the zuihitsu style. The point is to study issues and attitudes in a particular place and time – not so different from some of what I've discussed about a travel journal, right?

The American Society of Poets considers the literary form a hybrid form that amounts to a "prose poem." Which is only fitting, since in the original Pillow Book of Sei Shonagon, she includes a number of types of writing including 164 lists, such as "Elegant things" and "Things that cannot be compared."

These lists show us a rounded person – but the gossipy tone and weight of the events going on at Court give the overall narrative substance. I guess the point is, you never know when you begin a journal what it might lead up to. Keeping a travel journal from the beginning of a journey lets you record clearly events you would not necessarily be able to recall clearly otherwise by the time you realize they are important.

By the same token, you don't know what will happen later in life that might make your current journal more interesting. For example:

> "During the 1600s in London Samuel Pepys began keeping a journal to document his financial progress, but as his career progressed, it grew to encompass every aspect of his life, from dalliances to matters of state. His diary covered events such as his appointment as Chief Secretary to the Admiralty and his account of the Great Fire of London." – Journal Keeping: How to Use Reflective Writing for Effective Learning

So maybe you do take a trip to Iceland, and it sparks a whole new direction in your life. Looking back at the travel journal you kept on that initial trip could be priceless.

Sometimes, though, a trip isn't lifechanging. It's just part of what we've done and who we are. There's a whole tradition of journaling just to share with family and friends. They also allow us to share information that will be of later interest to our families or communities. For example, pioneer-era women recorded births, deaths and everything in between in detailed journals that they expected to be read by others and cherished as family keepsakes. If travel is part of your personal legacy, you will definitely want journals you can share, in conjunction with ephemera and photos.

For creatives, journals are common ways to feed creativity, with journaling projects that include free-writing about why certain themes are important to the writer, personal history to explore, and ideas for fiction. Other creatives have kept journals about their process and their lives. Writers such as Franz Kafka, Leo Tolstoy, Virginia Wolfe, and Sylvia Plath all have significant journals.

If you're a writer, poet or musician, you can use your travel journal to record snippets of overheard dialogue, and how new ideas you're encountering juxtapose with your previous work. Sometimes a change in perspective can solve plot problems or give you an image that will form a powerful symbol. You could even jot a poem or a piece of flash fiction (less than 1,000 words) at the beginning of each journal entry.

Journaling to Plan

Before you even leave for your trip, your travel journal serves as a place to organize information for your upcoming trip – and those to follow. Since you will likely have the journal on you as you go, it makes a handy place to jot down itineraries and confirmation numbers. (Just be careful not to misplace your journal, and consider having a digital backup copy of pages that have important information, just in case. If you plan to take your travel journal anywhere rugged, make sure to store it in a waterproof bag.)

There are prompts in this journal that allow you to look at what you already know about a place to build anticipation for the actual visit. It can also serve as a place to gather notes about spots you want to visit and things you want to do while at a destination. There are also prompts to help you summarize the experience upon your return. The journal then becomes a pre and post trip organizational tool.

Keeping a travel journal lets you record impressions of places and experiences that will help you decide where else to travel next – and which types of travel just weren't for you.

Journaling to Remember

Like flipping through an old photo album, looking at past journal entries can remind you of details of long-ago trips that you might otherwise have forgotten. Try to record the quirky parts of your journey that will make for good memories later. Include any epiphanies you had about life or the world. Also try to record the names of places you go and people you meet. Did you pet a cute dog or see a farm cat blinking in the sun? Eat the best eggplant parmesan you've ever had? Have sushi at a fish market? These may seem like small moments when they happen, but trust me, you will want to remember them later.

Journaling to Tell Stories

At its heart, journaling is about storytelling, whether you are telling the stories to yourself or sharing them with others. This means the more you journal, the more you practice telling stories in an inviting and vivid way. You can experiment with writing technique and format, learning more about the written word. Who knows? It may make you smoother at in-person speaking too, as you are prepared to answer questions from friends and family about your trip.

Travel itself enhances creativity, as you are exposed to different ways of thinking. Psychologists and neuroscientists have actually started studying the link between creativity, neuroplasticity and traveling/living in new environments. Our brains are forced to process a barrage of information, forging new neural pathways and making different connections between information. This is all great for sparking story ideas.

Don't be shy about asking questions along the way. People generally love talking about their favorite things. You can ask for food recommendations, or ask an artist about the processes involved. You can often also get deeper insights into culture, history and local landmarks.

Take time to exercise your creativity, too. Maybe you want to make up backstory for the people you net that day and write a short story about them. Maybe a scenic vista has inspired you to write poetry or a song. Include an illustrated map or a sketch, if the mood takes you.

As far as the writing itself, focus on clarity over literary gimmicks or flowery language. This means short sentences, short paragraphs, strong verbs, and concrete imagery. Explain jargon and write out acronyms the first time you use them. You want your reader to feel up to speed, and that can include adding in context that seems obvious to you. This even applies if you plan to share your journal as a family legacy project. Your kids may know who Great Aunt Jessica is, but their grandkids will have no idea. Background information goes toward the end of your entry, so that it doesn't distract from the flow of the story or bore readers who already know these details.

Even if your journal is just for you, it presents a great opportunity to improve your writing skills.

Writing about People

When you journal, you put yourself in the place of the natator and become the main character of the piece. When you write about people you meet as you travel, if you want them to be vivid in your readers' minds, you have to render them the same way you would a fictional character in a story. This means picking a main trait to show in your journal entry. Yes, people are complex and have multiple sides to them, but there is usually a main trait present at any given moment. You didn't just meet a mime stuck in an imaginary box on the street. You met a bored mime repeatedly checking his watch. That could signal impatience – or anticipation. What vibe did you actually get in the moment? What trait did you feel was at the person's core?

To make a person feel unique, look for interesting details:

Capture bits of dialogue – The way a person speaks says a lot about them. Especially note their regional words for common items.

What did the person look like? – You don't need an extensive description, just a few details.

What piece of clothing or accessory feels "iconic" – This can basically become a symbol for the person in your journaling.

What kind of shoes did the person have on? – You can tell a lot about a person's lifestyle from their footwear choices.

What did this person actually want? – Out of life or in the moment. Did this impact you?

What makes the person important enough for you to want to include them in your journal?

Writing about Place

The depth you go into describing the scenery you are passing through, or the particulars of a city you are visiting, will depend on the purpose of your journal. If you're a birdwatcher or into plants, you may want to record every unique thing you see.

If you are more trying to record your thoughts and feelings about being in a new place, just sprinkle in enough details to remind you of the landscape. Look for specifics that have meaning, either to you or culturally. If you are in Japan, which side of the escalator is everyone riding on? (It makes a different which area you are in.) Sometimes what isn't there can be the most intriguing. When we last visited Japan, we crossed the Shibuya Scramble (known for being the busiest intersection in the world) in the middle of the day, and there was hardly anyone there. We were on our way to see the nearby Hachiko Statue (since my husband is a huge animal lover, and it is such a poignant story, of the Akita dog waiting at the station every day for a master who had passed away), and I was bracing myself for walking through so many people. The anti-climax of the empty intersection was quite memorable.

To flesh out a setting for your journal entry:

Make a list of the details that stand out in your mind. Circle the ones that seem most unique to the place you have visited.

Contrast the place you are at with your home. What is the most different? Is there anything you feel is an improvement?

Look for details that you have an emotional connection to. Is a mountain so majestic you want to cry? Is being in a car on the "wrong" side of the street intimidating? Are you falling in love with walking down a particular street, stopping at a particular shop?

What is the weather like? Has it changed over the course of your trip? Is that worth noting in this particular entry?

What will you miss about the destination once you return home?

Writing about Food

"Never eat the same meal twice. If you want to be knowledgeable about food, you need to experience it yourself."
– Amanda Hesser (Food 52)

There's definitely a difference in the way you write about food if your journal is just for yourself, or if you want to share the highlights of your trip with others by sharing food pics and recipes. If you are writing just for yourself, focus on what the experience of the meal means to you. Was this a bucket-list restaurant you finally got to visit? Or an unexpected delight you never realized you needed to try? Was the food new to you? Or something that made you feel unexpectedly at home in a new place?

Food connects us in unexpected ways. For instance, almost everywhere in the world there's a rice dish. There's also probably a variation on coffee or tea. By understanding what people eat and why, you get a little glimpse into who they are. Maybe your journal entry about it can help you discover why you chose this particular destination to travel to.

If your intent is to share your entries, you still need to be somewhat personal because food is inherently a personal topic. The only way to share the experience you had with a particular food is to give personal impressions. It often helps to share your connection with the food. I've written in a couple of posts about how Community Coffee specifically reminds me of my grandmother's house, and of family. That one detail helps ground a lot of what I say about coffee in general, no matter where in the world I'm drinking it. If the food and culture is completely new to you, admit that, and express what you especially enjoyed about the experience. Perhaps talk about something you learned, about a particular ingredient or a cooking technique. Include the recipes, if you have them. Test those recipes multiple times first.

To deepen your writing about the food:

Find a connection between your life and the food you're presenting. What makes this food meaningful? Why did you choose to make this and not something else?

Focus on the five senses – how would you describe the way parsley smells or the way chocolate tastes? What does it sound like when you open the Dutch oven on a roasting chicken?

Put the food in context. Talk about the restaurant or street stall or person's home where you enjoyed it.

Write about the food as part of a larger experience. Was the meal punctuated by deep conversation, or did it come after a long day of hiking? Give us those connections.

Writing about Self

Your journal can become your main tool for self-reflection during your trip. You have chosen to go on a journey for a reason. What was it? Are you celebrating a new chapter in your life? Healing from a loss? Accompanying friends? Pulling yourself out of your comfort zone to try something new? Revisiting a place you haven't seen in a long time? Taking an annual trip?

Writing allows you to process thoughts and emotions in a way that sometimes allows you to stop dwelling on them. Thus, journaling can be healing, especially if an experience unexpectedly brings up un-healed pain from the past. You can sometimes put it down on paper to consider later, after you enjoy the rest of your trip. If you have more to say, you may even decide to journal between trips. Some even journal daily, to promote creativity and process emotion.

Travel, and recording your thoughts on it, can help you see how your perspective has changed over time, as you look back at each trip, and what you thought was new or challenging.

To deepen your writing about self:

Look at yourself as the protagonist of your journal. Protagonists usually have an internal growth arc and an external story arc. You could be stepping into an unfamiliar place to fuel self-discovery and personal improvement.

Allow yourself to free associate. You never know where the associations will take you, and you may hit on something you really needed to write about.

Be honest on the page, even if it is difficult.

Write about positive emotional reactions during your trip. What did you need about this trip, emotionally? What about it is healing?

Choosing an Audience

Will you share the journal with others, perhaps as a legacy for family? Will you use it to prepare articles, blog posts or vlogs? Or is it just for you, to record private observations? Deciding this in advance will help you focus on how you want to approach the journal, and how personal you want to get while writing entries. If a journal is just for you, you can bare personal hurts and secrets without having to worry about editing them out later. This can promote a deeper freedom for self-discovery.

On the other hand, if you plan to share your entries, you can write them with an article-style structure in mind, minimizing the need to re-work the information. You might even land somewhere between the two, writing for yourself, but later reworking the best parts into articles you plan to share through traditional outlets or on blogs or vlogs.

If you are sharing your work, you have to consider who will be interested in reading it. Travel blogs do better if there is a focus. You may want to center your travels around a particular hobby or type of exploration. Since I write fiction that deals with chocolate and coffee, I often frame travels to a new place around exploring the local coffee and chocolate scene. But your focus could be anything – snorkeling, hiking, shopping. I've known people who traveled specifically to eat at restaurants covered on Diners, Drive-Ins and Dives. And others who travel birding trails, maybe even hoping for a Big Year. These types of activities center a journal, giving the potential for the whole thing to take on a greater meaning as you explore WHY you are drawn to the activity and to the people involved. (Think something like Julie and Julia, where a blogger decides to chronicle cooking her way through Julia Child's cookbook. She set a challenge and showed what she learned from it. Travel can offer the same kind of challenge.)

Sensory Writing

Details that appeal to the five senses (plus the kinesthetic sense) tend to make for stronger writing. That's because if you put a reader in the scene, it lights up the parts of the brain that want to believe a situation is really happening. Tell us about the catch in your breathing, and we'll feel it too.

Most journal writers naturally include sight (unless they have an impairment). If you're writing about a beach, you will probably include the bluer than blue water, the flecked sand, the colors of the sunset. But think about the other senses. What did you hear on that beach? What smell was in the air? What did that sand actually feel like against your feet – coarse and flaky or soft and fine?

As you journal, choose details that appeal to different senses. Experiment in your journal entries with trying to include at least three different senses in varying places in each piece. This is especially beneficial if you want to share your travels with an audience, due to different learning styles. Describing yourself in motion or doing something at the beginning of an entry will draw in a kinesthetic learner. Dialogue early in the piece will appeal to an auditory learner. Tying something visual in as a symbol will appeal to a visual learner.

Balancing this will help you write concrete, relatable journal entries. Intersperse your thoughts and emotions between the sensory bits, and you will have something powerful.

Avoid abstractions whenever possible.

Don't just say, "He was kind." Show him buying a tire for you when you got stranded on the highway.

Don't just say, "She was sad." Show us the expression on her face and the way she's covered the floor with the wads of Kleenex from blowing her nose.

This ties into the idea of showing rather than telling, an important concept for fiction writers that also applies to journaling. It's impossible to show every single thing in your journal entry. TELL us the overviews and connecting events, but slow down and really SHOW us the important events in your journey.

Involuntary Autobiographical Memory

Often we hesitate to write our memories because we're not sure they're accurate or objective. We're afraid we can't remember details even for the time it takes to finish a day of travel and sit down to write about it. Let alone if we want to reference something that happened years or decades ago.

Keep in mind -- There is no such thing as "correct" memories. If half a dozen people view a fender bender, they are each going to have a different perception of exactly what happened, based on who they are and what they were focusing on. You can be honest about not being sure if you're remembering something correctly. You just need to avoid flat-out fabrication (a la the James Frey A Million Little Pieces scandal).

While you travel, don't be surprised if you unexpectedly come across a smell, taste or sound that sparks a memory. This phenomenon is called Involuntary Autobiographical Memory. It was first discussed by Marcel Proust, writing in his massive novel In Search of Lost Time. His main character dunks a madeleine in a cup of tea and is mentally transported back to childhood. It's the same phenomenon where a specific song comes on the radio, and you flash back to being a teenager, or to a specific time you danced with someone you care about. It's called involuntary, because you weren't trying to remember anything, and you can't stop it. Including genuine IAMs in your journal can give you the opportunity to write about deeply ingrained memories.

Journaling Quickly to Stay in the Moment

One of the most challenging parts of travel journaling is keeping up the journal over a long trip – or over a lifetime. Don't overthink things, or you could wind up spending a significant part of your trip writing and re-writing. Unless you're posting the journal entries live as you travel, save the editing for when you get home.

Ideally, you would want to write every day of the trip, but if that isn't feasible, at least make notes of important names, numbers and other details.

Rather than trying to record everything, all day long, get down the highlights. Choose vivid, striking details that will put readers in the scene – or that will transport you back in time, if your journal is just for you. Choose what is most important – the external record of events or the way you felt in a given place and make sure you have complete information on that aspect.

You can actually use the act of journaling to be more in the moment. Focus on the present moment, and be mindful about what you are experiencing, and you will be more prepared for sensory writing, using those all important details to be able to recreate the scene. This will also improve your observational skills as you practice journaling over time. A heightened awareness of your surroundings, and looking for the all-important WHY of your experience can lead to a more meaningful trip.

Don't forget to stop and just BE in the amazing places you've worked so hard to get to. On one of our trips to Hawaii, we camped on Kilauea, which had been a bucket list item for me for a long time. I spent a good bit of time trying to take pics of the lava flows down in the crater. But the most memorable part for me was when I just sat down at the edge, with the leftovers of a bag of spicy hurricane popcorn that I had bought at the previous day's night market, and sat quietly with my husband, marveling at the scale of it all.

Including Ephemera

There is no one right way to journal. Some people enjoy pasting in ephemera, such as playbills or ticket stubs. Others like to add pressed leaves or flowers from the travel location, tucked into the pages of the journal.

You could use stickers, or other items available from the scrapbook aisle of your local craft store, to decorate the pages of your journal.

This is part of what makes each travel journal such a unique, creative souvenir.

Your Journal -- Tools and Journal Entries

Why I Travel Self-Inventory

What types of travel do I want to do?
(Mountains vs Beaches, Urban vs. Nature, etc.)

My Travel goals:
(Examples: Explore a foreign country/my home country. Visit an iconic city. Explore coffee shops around the world. Snorkel significant reefs, see endangered wildlife habitats.)

How do I like to travel?
(Road trips? Cruise ships? Organized tours? Impulsive Destinations?)

What do I want to get out of my travel?

Dream destinations bucket list.

I really want to see:

Historical Landmarks:

Art and Culture Destinations:

Hidden Gems and Off the Beaten Path Destinations:

Eco Tourism Goals:

Culinary Tourism Goals:

Wildlife Destinations:

Adventure Destinations:

Aquatic Destinations:

Global Destinations:

    Countries I have a connection to:

    Countries I've always wanted to explore:

    Wonders of the World:

    Islands:

    Mountains:

US Destinations:

    Places I have a connection to:

    Cities I've always wanted to explore:

    State/National Parks:

    Road-Side Stops:

Statement of Intention

I am writing this journal because:

I want the style of this journal to be:
(Examples: A record? Notes for a larger project? A hobby akin to scrapbooking?)

I plan to share this journal with:
(Examples: It's just for me. Close friends and family. I want to publish pieces of it.)

A theme or goal I have for my travel endeavors? An activity or task I want to center my travel around?
(Examples: Personal growth, social issues, food exploration.)

What goals do I have for my journaling process?
(Ex. Write every day of my trip. Visit an art museum each day and record my favorite painting. See a new marine animal each day and use it as a theme for the journal entry.)

Using Imagery

Take a moment to be aware of where you are. Make brief notes about the inputs you feel for each of your senses, and incorporate them into the narration of your next journal entry.

I can see . . .	I can hear . . .	I can touch . . .
I can smell . . .	I can taste . . .	Descriptive words that come to mind are . . .
My body moves . . .	I feel (hunger, pain, etc.) . . .	My reaction is . . .

Use at least two sensory inputs to write an introductory sentence.

Observation Skill Prompts

Take a few moments to jot notes about your location. Use them to add specifics to your next journal entry.

Is this an urban or rural area?

How are people dressed?

Is there a person who really stands out? How would you describe this individual?

What business is conducted in this place? Or what is grown/produced?

If there are stores, where are people going and what do they come out with?

What in this environment catches my eye?

What is next to it?

Look at the ground and/or pavement. What does this tell me about the place?

Look up at the rooftops, sky, and surrounding buildings. What does this tell me about the place?

Where is the lighting coming from if at night?

What are the street names nearby? What are the businesses called?

If I ordered food or drink, what were the dishes called, and what was the name of the chef? Of the restaurant?

If I near a park or beach, what is it called and who/what is it named for? What flora and fauna are present?

If there is a nearby landmark what is it called? Is it something I would want to visit?

Journal Prompts

Not sure what to write about on a given day? Here are some prompts to get you started.

1. What is important about the architecture in the place I am are visiting?
2. Are there billboards or other advertisements allowed in the place I are visiting?
3. Have I tried any foods that take me out of my comfort zone?
4. Did anything bring me joy?
5. Did I experience art? How did I react emotionally?
6. What unexpected challenges did I face?
7. What travel tips would I give someone going to the place I am visiting?
8. Did I gain any cultural insights?
9. Are there any public spaces or parks? What did I learn about who these spaces are named for?
10. What did I appreciate about the landscape?
11. What is the history of the place I am visiting?
12. Is there something unique about the place I am staying?
13. Am I doing luxury or budge travel? Is this my usual style?
14. What fellow travelers have I met along the way?
15. Did someone say something memorable today?
16. Did I learn a new word or a new regional way of expressing a concept?
17. What animals have I seen on this trip?
18. Have I read any books set in this place? If so, how do they measure up to the real thing?

19. Have I read any books or seen any films created by someone from this place? If so, how did they affect my impressions?
20. Did I make someone feel good about themselves today?
21. What souvenirs am I bringing home?
22. Write a pretend postcard to a friend.
23. What was my favorite outfit I've worn on my trip?
24. Is there a song I associate with the place I am visiting?
25. What would I be doing today if I weren't traveling?
26. How does this trip compare to others 've been on?
27. What was the first thing I noticed when you arrived at my destination?
28. How did it feel waking up at a new place?
29. Did anything in the place I am visiting remind me of home?
30. Did I bring a book to read while I am traveling? If so, what is it and why?
31. What made me laugh today?
32. What did I pack but wind up not needing?
33. Am I different in some way while traveling? (A morning person? Less self-conscious?)
34. How do I want my life to be different when I get home?
35. Did I connect with nature in some way today?
36. What did I love about the city I traveled through today?
37. What made me feel connected to the world today?
38. What made me feel like I experienced personal growth today?

Destination	Language
Date	Time Zone
Currency	Weather

Have you been here before? What previous notions of this place do you have?
What are you looking forward to?
What will take you out of your comfort zone?
Planned activities and reservation numbers
Questions to ask
To do list

_____

_____

_____

_____

_____

How did you feel in this place?
Who did you meet?
Where did you go?
Where did you eat?
Highlights
Discoveries and surprises

Destination	Language
Date	Time Zone
Currency	Weather

Have you been here before? What previous notions of this place do you have?
What are you looking forward to?
What will take you out of your comfort zone?
Planned activities and reservation numbers
Questions to ask
To do list

_____

_____

_____

_____

_____

How did you feel in this place?
Who did you meet?
Where did you go?
Where did you eat?
Highlights
Discoveries and surprises

Destination	Language
Date	Time Zone
Currency	Weather

Have you been here before? What previous notions of this place do you have?
What are you looking forward to?
What will take you out of your comfort zone?
Planned activities and reservation numbers
Questions to ask
To do list

_____

_____

_____

_____

_____

How did you feel in this place?
Who did you meet?
Where did you go?
Where did you eat?
Highlights
Discoveries and surprises

Destination	Language
Date	Time Zone
Currency	Weather

Have you been here before? What previous notions of this place do you have?

What are you looking forward to?

What will take you out of your comfort zone?

Planned activities and reservation numbers

Questions to ask

To do list

_____

_____

_____

_____

_____

How did you feel in this place?
Who did you meet?
Where did you go?
Where did you eat?
Highlights
Discoveries and surprises

Destination	Language
Date	Time Zone
Currency	Weather

Have you been here before? What previous notions of this place do you have?
What are you looking forward to?
What will take you out of your comfort zone?
Planned activities and reservation numbers
Questions to ask
To do list

_____

_____

_____

_____

_____

How did you feel in this place?
Who did you meet?
Where did you go?
Where did you eat?
Highlights
Discoveries and surprises

Destination	Language
Date	Time Zone
Currency	Weather

Have you been here before? What previous notions of this place do you have?
What are you looking forward to?
What will take you out of your comfort zone?
Planned activities and reservation numbers
Questions to ask
To do list

How did you feel in this place?	
Who did you meet?	
Where did you go?	
Where did you eat?	
Highlights	
Discoveries and surprises	

Destination	Language
Date	Time Zone
Currency	Weather

Have you been here before? What previous notions of this place do you have?
What are you looking forward to?
What will take you out of your comfort zone?
Planned activities and reservation numbers
Questions to ask
To do list

_____

_____

_____

_____

_____

How did you feel in this place?
Who did you meet?
Where did you go?
Where did you eat?
Highlights
Discoveries and surprises

Destination	Language
Date	Time Zone
Currency	Weather

Have you been here before? What previous notions of this place do you have?
What are you looking forward to?
What will take you out of your comfort zone?
Planned activities and reservation numbers
Questions to ask
To do list

_____

_____

_____

_____

_____

How did you feel in this place?
Who did you meet?
Where did you go?
Where did you eat?
Highlights
Discoveries and surprises

Destination	Language
Date	Time Zone
Currency	Weather

Have you been here before? What previous notions of this place do you have?
What are you looking forward to?
What will take you out of your comfort zone?
Planned activities and reservation numbers
Questions to ask
To do list

_____

_____

_____

_____

How did you feel in this place?
Who did you meet?
Where did you go?
Where did you eat?
Highlights
Discoveries and surprises

Destination	Language
Date	Time Zone
Currency	Weather

Have you been here before? What previous notions of this place do you have?
What are you looking forward to?
What will take you out of your comfort zone?
Planned activities and reservation numbers
Questions to ask
To do list

_____

_____

_____

_____

_____

How did you feel in this place?
Who did you meet?
Where did you go?
Where did you eat?
Highlights
Discoveries and surprises

Destination	Language
Date	Time Zone
Currency	Weather

Have you been here before? What previous notions of this place do you have?
What are you looking forward to?
What will take you out of your comfort zone?
Planned activities and reservation numbers
Questions to ask
To do list

_____

_____

_____

_____

_____

How did you feel in this place?
Who did you meet?
Where did you go?
Where did you eat?
Highlights
Discoveries and surprises

Destination	Language
Date	Time Zone
Currency	Weather

Have you been here before? What previous notions of this place do you have?
What are you looking forward to?
What will take you out of your comfort zone?
Planned activities and reservation numbers
Questions to ask
To do list

_____

_____

_____

_____

How did you feel in this place?
Who did you meet?
Where did you go?
Where did you eat?
Highlights
Discoveries and surprises

Destination	Language
Date	Time Zone
Currency	Weather

Have you been here before? What previous notions of this place do you have?
What are you looking forward to?
What will take you out of your comfort zone?
Planned activities and reservation numbers
Questions to ask
To do list

_____

_____

_____

_____

_____

How did you feel in this place?

Who did you meet?

Where did you go?

Where did you eat?

Highlights

Discoveries and surprises

Destination	Language
Date	Time Zone
Currency	Weather

Have you been here before? What previous notions of this place do you have?
What are you looking forward to?
What will take you out of your comfort zone?
Planned activities and reservation numbers
Questions to ask
To do list

_____

_____

_____

_____

_____

How did you feel in this place?
Who did you meet?
Where did you go?
Where did you eat?
Highlights
Discoveries and surprises

Destination	Language
Date	Time Zone
Currency	Weather

Have you been here before? What previous notions of this place do you have?
What are you looking forward to?
What will take you out of your comfort zone?
Planned activities and reservation numbers
Questions to ask
To do list

_____

_____

_____

_____

_____

How did you feel in this place?
Who did you meet?
Where did you go?
Where did you eat?
Highlights
Discoveries and surprises

Destination	Language
Date	Time Zone
Currency	Weather

Have you been here before? What previous notions of this place do you have?
What are you looking forward to?
What will take you out of your comfort zone?
Planned activities and reservation numbers
Questions to ask
To do list

_____

_____

_____

_____

_____

How did you feel in this place?
Who did you meet?
Where did you go?
Where did you eat?
Highlights
Discoveries and surprises

Destination	Language
Date	Time Zone
Currency	Weather

Have you been here before? What previous notions of this place do you have?
What are you looking forward to?
What will take you out of your comfort zone?
Planned activities and reservation numbers
Questions to ask
To do list

___

___

___

___

___

How did you feel in this place?
Who did you meet?
Where did you go?
Where did you eat?
Highlights
Discoveries and surprises

Destination	Language
Date	Time Zone
Currency	Weather

Have you been here before? What previous notions of this place do you have?
What are you looking forward to?
What will take you out of your comfort zone?
Planned activities and reservation numbers
Questions to ask
To do list

_____

_____

_____

_____

_____

How did you feel in this place?
Who did you meet?
Where did you go?
Where did you eat?
Highlights
Discoveries and surprises

Destination	Language
Date	Time Zone
Currency	Weather

Have you been here before? What previous notions of this place do you have?
What are you looking forward to?
What will take you out of your comfort zone?
Planned activities and reservation numbers
Questions to ask
To do list

_____

_____

_____

_____

_____

How did you feel in this place?
Who did you meet?
Where did you go?
Where did you eat?
Highlights
Discoveries and surprises

Destination	Language
Date	Time Zone
Currency	Weather

Have you been here before? What previous notions of this place do you have?
What are you looking forward to?
What will take you out of your comfort zone?
Planned activities and reservation numbers
Questions to ask
To do list

_____

_____

_____

_____

_____

How did you feel in this place?
Who did you meet?
Where did you go?
Where did you eat?
Highlights
Discoveries and surprises

Destination	Language
Date	Time Zone
Currency	Weather

Have you been here before? What previous notions of this place do you have?
What are you looking forward to?
What will take you out of your comfort zone?
Planned activities and reservation numbers
Questions to ask
To do list

_____

_____

_____

_____

_____

How did you feel in this place?
Who did you meet?
Where did you go?
Where did you eat?
Highlights
Discoveries and surprises

Destination	Language
Date	Time Zone
Currency	Weather

Have you been here before? What previous notions of this place do you have?
What are you looking forward to?
What will take you out of your comfort zone?
Planned activities and reservation numbers
Questions to ask
To do list

_____

_____

_____

_____

_____

How did you feel in this place?	
Who did you meet?	
Where did you go?	
Where did you eat?	
Highlights	
Discoveries and surprises	

Destination	Language
Date	Time Zone
Currency	Weather

Have you been here before? What previous notions of this place do you have?
What are you looking forward to?
What will take you out of your comfort zone?
Planned activities and reservation numbers
Questions to ask
To do list

_____

_____

_____

_____

_____

How did you feel in this place?
Who did you meet?
Where did you go?
Where did you eat?
Highlights
Discoveries and surprises

Destination	Language
Date	Time Zone
Currency	Weather

Have you been here before? What previous notions of this place do you have?
What are you looking forward to?
What will take you out of your comfort zone?
Planned activities and reservation numbers
Questions to ask
To do list

_____

_____

_____

_____

_____

How did you feel in this place?
Who did you meet?
Where did you go?
Where did you eat?
Highlights
Discoveries and surprises

Destination	Language
Date	Time Zone
Currency	Weather

Have you been here before? What previous notions of this place do you have?
What are you looking forward to?
What will take you out of your comfort zone?
Planned activities and reservation numbers
Questions to ask
To do list

_____

_____

_____

_____

_____

How did you feel in this place?
Who did you meet?
Where did you go?
Where did you eat?
Highlights
Discoveries and surprises

Destination	Language
Date	Time Zone
Currency	Weather

Have you been here before? What previous notions of this place do you have?
What are you looking forward to?
What will take you out of your comfort zone?
Planned activities and reservation numbers
Questions to ask
To do list

How did you feel in this place?
Who did you meet?
Where did you go?
Where did you eat?
Highlights
Discoveries and surprises

Destination	Language
Date	Time Zone
Currency	Weather

Have you been here before? What previous notions of this place do you have?
What are you looking forward to?
What will take you out of your comfort zone?
Planned activities and reservation numbers
Questions to ask
To do list

_____

_____

_____

_____

_____

How did you feel in this place?
Who did you meet?
Where did you go?
Where did you eat?
Highlights
Discoveries and surprises

Destination	Language
Date	Time Zone
Currency	Weather

Have you been here before? What previous notions of this place do you have?
What are you looking forward to?
What will take you out of your comfort zone?
Planned activities and reservation numbers
Questions to ask
To do list

_____

_____

_____

_____

_____

How did you feel in this place?
Who did you meet?
Where did you go?
Where did you eat?
Highlights
Discoveries and surprises

Destination	Language
Date	Time Zone
Currency	Weather

Have you been here before? What previous notions of this place do you have?
What are you looking forward to?
What will take you out of your comfort zone?
Planned activities and reservation numbers
Questions to ask
To do list

_____

_____

_____

_____

_____

How did you feel in this place?
Who did you meet?
Where did you go?
Where did you eat?
Highlights
Discoveries and surprises

Destination	Language
Date	Time Zone
Currency	Weather

Have you been here before? What previous notions of this place do you have?
What are you looking forward to?
What will take you out of your comfort zone?
Planned activities and reservation numbers
Questions to ask
To do list

_____

_____

_____

_____

_____

How did you feel in this place?
Who did you meet?
Where did you go?
Where did you eat?
Highlights
Discoveries and surprises

Destination	Language
Date	Time Zone
Currency	Weather

Have you been here before? What previous notions of this place do you have?
What are you looking forward to?
What will take you out of your comfort zone?
Planned activities and reservation numbers
Questions to ask
To do list

_____

_____

_____

_____

_____

How did you feel in this place?
Who did you meet?
Where did you go?
Where did you eat?
Highlights
Discoveries and surprises

Destination	Language
Date	Time Zone
Currency	Weather

Have you been here before? What previous notions of this place do you have?
What are you looking forward to?
What will take you out of your comfort zone?
Planned activities and reservation numbers
Questions to ask
To do list

_____

_____

_____

_____

_____

How did you feel in this place?
Who did you meet?
Where did you go?
Where did you eat?
Highlights
Discoveries and surprises

Destination	Language
Date	Time Zone
Currency	Weather

Have you been here before? What previous notions of this place do you have?
What are you looking forward to?
What will take you out of your comfort zone?
Planned activities and reservation numbers
Questions to ask
To do list

_____

_____

_____

_____

_____

How did you feel in this place?
Who did you meet?
Where did you go?
Where did you eat?
Highlights
Discoveries and surprises

Destination	Language
Date	Time Zone
Currency	Weather

Have you been here before? What previous notions of this place do you have?
What are you looking forward to?
What will take you out of your comfort zone?
Planned activities and reservation numbers
Questions to ask
To do list

_____

_____

_____

_____

_____

How did you feel in this place?
Who did you meet?
Where did you go?
Where did you eat?
Highlights
Discoveries and surprises

Destination	Language
Date	Time Zone
Currency	Weather

Have you been here before? What previous notions of this place do you have?
What are you looking forward to?
What will take you out of your comfort zone?
Planned activities and reservation numbers
Questions to ask
To do list

_____

_____

_____

_____

_____

How did you feel in this place?
Who did you meet?
Where did you go?
Where did you eat?
Highlights
Discoveries and surprises

Destination	Language
Date	Time Zone
Currency	Weather

Have you been here before? What previous notions of this place do you have?
What are you looking forward to?
What will take you out of your comfort zone?
Planned activities and reservation numbers
Questions to ask
To do list

_____

_____

_____

_____

_____

How did you feel in this place?
Who did you meet?
Where did you go?
Where did you eat?
Highlights
Discoveries and surprises

Destination	Language
Date	Time Zone
Currency	Weather

Have you been here before? What previous notions of this place do you have?
What are you looking forward to?
What will take you out of your comfort zone?
Planned activities and reservation numbers
Questions to ask
To do list

_____

_____

_____

_____

_____

How did you feel in this place?
Who did you meet?
Where did you go?
Where did you eat?
Highlights
Discoveries and surprises

Destination	Language
Date	Time Zone
Currency	Weather

Have you been here before? What previous notions of this place do you have?
What are you looking forward to?
What will take you out of your comfort zone?
Planned activities and reservation numbers
Questions to ask
To do list

_____

_____

_____

_____

_____

How did you feel in this place?
Who did you meet?
Where did you go?
Where did you eat?
Highlights
Discoveries and surprises

Destination	Language
Date	Time Zone
Currency	Weather

Have you been here before? What previous notions of this place do you have?
What are you looking forward to?
What will take you out of your comfort zone?
Planned activities and reservation numbers
Questions to ask
To do list

_____

_____

_____

_____

_____

How did you feel in this place?	
Who did you meet?	
Where did you go?	
Where did you eat?	
Highlights	
Discoveries and surprises	

Destination	Language
Date	Time Zone
Currency	Weather

Have you been here before? What previous notions of this place do you have?
What are you looking forward to?
What will take you out of your comfort zone?
Planned activities and reservation numbers
Questions to ask
To do list

_____

_____

_____

_____

_____

How did you feel in this place?
Who did you meet?
Where did you go?
Where did you eat?
Highlights
Discoveries and surprises

AMBER ROYER writes the CHOCOVERSE comic telenovela-style foodie-inspired space opera series (available from Angry Robot Books and Golden Tip Press). She is also co-author of the cookbook There are Herbs in My Chocolate, which combines culinary herbs and chocolate in over 60 sweet and savory recipes, and had a long-running column for Dave's Garden, where she covered gardening and crafting. She blogs about creative writing technique and all things chocolate related over at www.amberroyer.com. She also teaches creative writing in person in North Texas for UT Arlington Continuing Education. If you are very nice to her, she might make you cupcakes.

www.amberroyer.com Instagram: amberroyerauthor

www.ingramcontent.com/pod-product-compliance
Lightning Source LLC
Chambersburg PA
CBHW070057080526
44586CB00013B/1094